City Sonnets

Jonathan Bradley

THE CHOIR PRESS

First published in the United Kingdom in 2022 by

The Choir Press

ISBN 978-1-78963-334-4

For Harriet

The author

Jonathan Bradley has been writing poetry from an early age. This is his fourth book of poems to be published. The first two were of poems inspired by butterflies: *Papiliones* (Choir Press, 2017) and *A Kaleidoscope of Butterflies* (Merlin Unwin Books, 2020). His third, written jointly with his sister Jenny Bradley, was entitled *Sibling Poets: Travels through two lives – Fairy Path to Ha-Ha* (Choir Press, 2021). His poems and articles have been published in a number of other books and periodicals, including *The Alchemy Spoon*, *The Countryman*, and *Atropos*. A recently completed novel, *Bulls Bears and Bunfights* is awaiting publication, and a further collection of poetry is in preparation.

He is a Director of the War Poets Association and a member of the Council of the European Centre for Peace and Development. He divides his time between England and France and has travelled widely during a varied professional career in the academic world and in business.

Contents

Preface

The poems in this book were written at different times over a period of more than forty years. This may help to explain some of the differences between them of style and content. They were inspired by periods of my life spent living in several cities, including Durham, Marseille, Paris, Venice, Bristol, Oxford and London. Work and leisure travel have taken me also to many other cities on every continent except Antarctica. Some of the worst and the best aspects of human life can be seen in them. Although I now live in the country-side cities are still important in my life even though I prefer not to live in one.

The traditional sonnet form might seem an odd choice for this subject matter. It appeals to me because it is concise, has a long tradition in the literature of several languages and concentrates the mind of the author and the reader. My sonnets are written in the so-called Shakespearean form, with some occasional divergences. They are each fourteen lines long and consist of three rhyming quatrains in iambic pentameter with a final couplet. In most of them there occurs a 'volta' or turn, in which the subject matter illustrates a contradiction or shows a different perspective on the subject.

The verses in this book are not the perfect gems of the great Bard and I am all too conscious of their shortcomings. I felt that it was time to extract them from dog-eared notebooks and let them see the light of day. So here they are, and I offer them to the reader as poetic observations on aspects of modern city life, recounted in a time-honoured fashion.

City sonnets

City Bard

How dare I tread where Shakespeare chose to stride—
can I ignore four centuries of change?
Why with the time do I not glance aside
to new-found methods and to compounds strange?
Not just a lack of pride led me to choose
constraints that modern folk believe too tight,
but also sloth – an over-active muse
yields more than I can elegantly write;
So from this journal of a city man,
recorded in a noisy crowded mind,
are taken glimpses from a weekly span
selectively remembered and refined;
I hope that though he may find this mundane,
the greater poet's ghost will not complain.

Martin Droeshout Sculpsit London.

Addict

The fragments of her life are scattered wide—
her work, her marriage seem beyond repair,
depression, anguish where there once was pride.
Her beauty gone, she now has greasy hair,
swept back into a desperate pony tail
that stays askew, now prematurely grey;
her eyes are dull, her cheeks are sallow, pale
as if they never see the light of day.
A welcome fix eclipses all the pain,
the joyful needle in her waiting arm
distracts her from her days of mental rain
but pumps inside another dose of harm.
So now she struggles in a junk-filled pond;
her world has shrunk, she cannot see beyond.

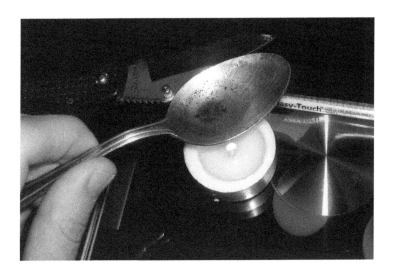

Beggar

The beggar who expects a little change
squats on the pavement with his metal dish;
his patient dog is rusty with the mange,
his clothing smells just slightly of old fish;
and terror slows my walk as I approach—
"he needs to eat, he has nowhere to sleep",
my mind's voice tells me, full of self-reproach,
but still my loathing for this man is deep
because he simply waits for charity…
Is he the kind they used to crucify?
If so, I know with awful clarity
how difficult it is to justify,
in my despair of kind psychopathy,
that I just cannot give him sympathy.

Book Group

This book group is a culture training ground
where educated ladies flex their minds;
there are a few who simply like the sound
of their own voice and some who hope to find
new friends or leave behind a boring spouse;
imagination links unlikely souls:
a teacher in her fair trade hand-made blouse,
a banker, writer, nurse, all share the bowls
of naughty nibbles, each one free to voice
their own reactions, focused through their lens,
enhanced or jaded by their wine of choice,
to judge the arduous work of others' pens.
A book may move, or even make them weep,
as long as they are not yet fast asleep.

Carnival

The meek and self-effacing have a chance
to show their face by putting on a mask
and reach for freedom, join a carefree dance
in rainbow gear, without the need to ask
permission from themselves to have some fun;
bright ostrich feathers help with a disguise,
releasing shaded souls into the sun
where colours sparkle, spirits stir and rise.
The pain of living in a filthy slum,
the filthy pain of suffering abuse—
they leave emotions paralysed and numb,
but mood can lift when dressed up as a moose.
Each lives a new persona for a day
Before they put their comic clothes away.

Cathedrals

Before they took majestic form in rock
cathedrals were a dream in human minds,
conceived not just to house a Christian flock;
the powerful and vain had them designed
to glorify their power and fame in life
and be remembered fondly after death—
a ruler could be laid beside his wife
in vaults so fine they took away their breath.
The architects are often now unknown
and never saw the miracles complete
around which urban streets and shops have grown,
where car parks, bars and banks lie at their feet.
And still they're here, as centuries have flown:
imagination fashioned into stone.

Cats

Disdainful, selfish, wilful, almost wild,
the city feral cat prowls every street,
his human neighbours now and then beguiled
by feline charm to throw him scraps of meat;
the loved has cuddles, and the hated, kicks—
depending on his luck he may waste lives:
a cat that likes to take a dish and licks
the butter gambles, yet for now he thrives.
But still he wants to hunt for flesh and blood,
and chases rodents, rabbits, voles and birds;
he hates the rain, and hides from wind and flood,
fastidious, he covers up his turds.
How much reduced would pleasure be for cats
deprived of chasing after city rats?

Cinema

Old picture houses suffered, squeezed between
insurgent television and sheer sloth,
but now a multi-coloured picture screen,
no longer silver, challenges them both
with armchair seats and meals on trays to eat
in comfort, planned by marketeers to make
the multi-sense experience complete,
illusions served with Earl Grey tea and cake.
An art-form reeled and then came from the brink
to rescue cinemas from bare neglect;
a few became a bingo hall or rink
but just enough avoided being wrecked.
Nostalgia, romance, horror, thriller kicks
are now restored in cities at the flicks.

Citizens

The highest, lowest, worst, the best all share
the flinty lands where buildings crowd and shove
to rise and jostle for refreshing air:
these city-dwellers seek a roof above
their sleeping, waking, working, lazing lives,
and every one dependent on the rest,
connected, though they're not just drones in hives
and have to be at other folks' behest.
The girl who helps an old man cross the road,
her mother in the park who plants a flower,
the man who clears the path when it has snowed—
collectively they wield a special power.
Inhabitants are not just denizens;
they share a civil life as citizens.

City Farm

A hippie mother in her ethnic shawl
has brought her girls to see a city farm;
she isn't sure they should be there at all—
it generates a conscientious qualm.
The ducks are cute, the lambs are very sweet,
the pigs and rabbits healthy and well fed,
yet some of them will soon end up as meat
entrancing while alive but tasty dead.
These children from an urban street are charmed
and never see the cruel countryside
where cash dictates what animals are farmed
and sentimental feelings cast aside.
The mother wonders when to scar their youth
by telling both her girls the nasty truth.

Commuter Train

An occult creature like an armoured eel
emerges from the gloom of shading night
and as it clatters closer turns to steel,
each staring eye a bright and glaring light.
The monster's flank disjoins from every gill
discharging travellers at the waiting line;
amorphous shoals of dense planktonic krill
commingle on the edge of platform nine.
The beast invades the tunnel with a bound
and morning papers rustle at the jolt:
commuters meekly hurtle through the ground
to storm the city in a dawn assault,
then eight hours later after work disperse
to start the same migration in reverse.

Concert Hall

They hold their virtual breath to see and hear
vibrating harmonies of ringing air
that through the ear can soon compose a tear
or chiming joy that soothes, dispels despair.
An audience makes tryst with those on stage
to share their love of song and so respond
as if to join in mutely and engage
in mutual pleasure, form a sensual bond.
Musicians sense this in the concert halls:
they need not see – it tingles and they feel;
a drifting murmur, rapture in the stalls
convey their message, make their listeners real.
Professional performers always know
they need an audience to have a show.

Corner Shop

Rashif Hussein was born and raised in Leeds
and never set a foot in Pakistan;
for many years he's served his locals' needs,
with rice and noodles, Sunblest White and Naan,
confectionery and incense sticks and drinks:
his mind has had to broaden over time
when locals asked for things with nods and winks,
he's even had his share of petty crime.
Some ruffians full of alcohol came round
to show they were the high and mighty race
but Rashif faced them down and stood his ground
while neighbours helped protect this vital place.
He might have suffered in an ethnic war
but locals fought to keep their corner store.

Councillor

A city ward can be a spoilt child
demanding sweets and special treats by right,
but when one person's pleased, another's riled,
what's day for one for someone else is night.
The parking outside Mrs Nichols's house
annoys her as she never finds a space
but Mr Browning has a different grouse:
he believes it is his rightful place.
The student house is full of boys and girls
who want to party, have some rowdy fun,
but neighbours hate the thumping night-time noise
and try to soak them with a water gun.
So how can council members win?
They try to help but sometimes just give in.

Delivery Driver

He never wonders why his van is white,
a colour seen as innocent by most;
his secret load is wrapped and out of sight,
each sender distant, cryptic, just a ghost.
He'd like to know what packages could hold,
although outside they all look much the same;
they might contain a bomb, or bars of gold,
but either way he has the praise or blame.
He has no truck with limits on his speed
and parks wherever visits make him stop.
To yellow lines and signs he pays no heed,
in haste to make an urgent parcel drop.
But still he knows his favourite bit of fun:
To ring the doorbell, turn and quickly run.

Demonstrator

To be alive, she knows, you should believe
in something that could make a better world:
reduce emissions, help the sick, relieve
distress, and so her banner is unfurled,
to stop a war, oppose the budget cuts—
each demonstration for a worthy cause,
with radical resolve, no ifs or buts,
no argument permitted to have flaws.
Although such fearsome problems grip her mind
her protests are a satisfying task,
displaying noisy passion to be kind
to other humans, even when unasked.
She doesn't stop to wonder if it's strange;
despite her efforts nothing much will change.

Dog-walker

The walker strides with several leads in hand,
aware of every canine wish, and care
to suit whatever owners might demand,
and give the dogs their favourite toothsome fare;
attentive always for a moment if
their precious charge has urgent need to pause,
to snuffle, dig, or take a longing sniff
with busy paws or gently drooling jaws,
at any passing canine on the way.
It's fun for all the dogs, who like the fuss,
but walkers have to do this every day
before they go to catch the evening bus.
So after that the dogs can sleep in peace
without becoming hopelessly obese.

Escape From a Pre-computer Office

The office clacks and shrills at quiet folk
as silent thought, reflection, count as sin;
the castigations – clatter, haste and smoke—
its victims cannot think in all the din.
When guilty lust for peace stirs up and pleads,
the firmest city creature's will grows weak
disabled by the body's urgent needs,
so then the trespasser creeps out to seek.
The bosses keep the still holes to themselves:
but one small place of rest remains exempt
and there no prying manager can delve
on pain of earning popular contempt.
Yet like a desk-job this serene retreat
is nothing more than paper and a seat.

Friday Night

A fever fills the streets on Friday nights
as heated spirits rise for the weekend,
and from the buses girls without their tights
collect in flocks to chatter and pretend
they couldn't care about the cool-guy boys
who eye them up and smile from café doors.
With vodka, lager, spirit shots, comes noise
from whirling dancers on the night-club floors
while later some, too drunk, will lose their poise
with screeches, whoops and alcoholic roars,
with lust and tears and unexpected joys
and charming boys converted into boors.
They sleep it off, until tomorrow, when,
it's time to go and do it all again.

From a Distance

The distant city steals along the vale,
a miniature, a model on display,
its lines and contours softened by a veil
of silver-rippling mist at break of day;
from here, on woodland heights, it may look tame,
a harmless plaything for a wandering eye,
its chimneys, streets, and factories free of blame
for lives so poisoned some of them will die.
But far from fields and woods, inside the town
the damage is much easier to see:
through hardship social peace can break right down
and homeless families struggle to be free.
Yet from the city all that can be seen
is sky and, underneath, some brown and green.

Ideal Estate

The planners had a vision of a place
where working folk could usefully be housed,
to be precision engineered, the face
of progress for a lucky people roused
from deference, looking for a better time;
then skinheads came and overturned the bins
while well-kept paths were strewn with filth and grime,
abandoned skips were filled with cast-off sins.
Some tidy model houses stood apart
as symbols of an artisan élite,
the rest were cheated of their brave new start
where mattresses were littering the street.
But here within penumbral city gloam
are many places people call their home.

Massage Parlour

The entrance looks like any other door
except there is a peephole in a slot;
it's not a place, of course, to find a whore—
the ladies here are simply fit and hot,
though some of them aren't sure where they are
because they left their village in the dark
when snatched from Poland in a smuggler's car.
And now the brutal choice they face is stark:
they try to flee, or sell their flesh for cash,
but there's a threatening Madam on the stair
and fear and shame preventing a quick dash
to freedom, so they have to stay on where
pathetic men whose lives are short of luck
find consolation in a casual fuck.

Monday

The armour of a woman or a man
is weakest on a certain mournful day,
when even plied with tea and cleansed with bran
they wish that time stood still and they could stay
in bed until the week's long dreams went by
without the stress of telephones or trains
and they could sleep their true life gliding high
above the fumes and other urban pains;
but earthly needs, the waking nightmares, win
and soon the City creature grows a crust,
a hardened shell to hide within—
in this protective jail they put their trust.
The second day of seven is the worst
and by crustaceans everywhere most cursed.

Le grand bailleur

Pandemic Ward

They keep arriving every viral day—
the sick and dying, gasping, full of dread;
arrivals may be filled with shocked dismay
to find the one next door already dead.
These anxious places are the borderlands
where stealthy raiders plunder human breath,
and every nurse or doctor understands
they too are near the no-man's land of death.
Some turn before they reach the border post,
but others must be rescued from the wire
before they catch a glimpse of their own ghost
by carers so committed they can't tire.
Each says a heartfelt thank you to their nurse,
relieved they won't be leaving in a hearse.

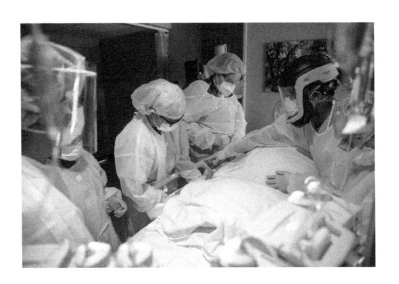

Parks

They're sometime remnants of a rural past
marooned amongst the bricks and concrete blocks,
a chance survival, never meant to last
yet now their lawns, geraniums and phlox,
their well-pruned trees and ornamental ponds
defy the fumes and creeping asphalt tide
with fragrant blooms and languid palm-tree fronds
affirming strong and verdant civic pride.
The mums with prams, the elderly on frames
enjoy the air, the benches and the flowers
while lively children run about their games
and stressed accountants rest in shady bowers.
A park pretends, a green impostor place
yet still gives peace in its illusive space.

Rats

They stick to family values in their home,
their many offspring brought up to be tough,
but when they're on the streets allowed to roam
then life becomes a struggle, hard and rough,
so education comes in heavy blows
escaping down a stinking city drain
or, injured, left to die as food for crows:
survivors seem oblivious to pain.
They have no doctors, pensions or address,
no nurseries, care homes, savings in the bank,
their homes are always in a filthy mess
and yet they thrive in hovels rank and dank.
So how would cities cope with all the rats
without the hunting skills of feral cats?

Refuse

We don't discard the things we truly love
unless they're too addictive to be kept
in secret drawers or guilty shelves above
the wardrobe, near the bed where once you slept
with dreams that showed you how to throw away
bad habits with the greasy kitchen trash;
perhaps you felt more virtuous for a day—
at least you saved a little vicious cash.
Around the town remains of breakfast baps,
their plastic wrappers thrown away in haste,
old socks, used needles, fag ends, mealtime scraps
accumulate as needless human waste.
When dustmen empty out the rubbish bins
they clear, but don't forgive, a city's sins.

Rough Sleeper

Rough sleepers aren't an urban myth; they're real,
on doorsteps, under arches, on the street
and often worried where to find a meal,
with aching limbs and painful feet.
But some of these forgotten people think
they'd rather be at large than in a slum
(or else there is no further down to sink),
it's better, even if their toes are numb.
So, bit by bit, they leave their souls elsewhere,
becoming pavement litter, tossed aside.
They don't expect a passer-by to care,
and anyway no longer try to hide.
You shouldn't need to sleep beneath a tree
to lead a life that's spirited and free.

Rule by Bells

With apologies to the memory of John Betjeman

The bells call children from the playing-ground
and summon ageing poets to their rest;
in varied pitch and tone their accents sound
from end to end of every human quest;
in joy or sorrow, peace or war they sing,
prepared at first by artifice of men
who cast the church bells long before they swing
and fix the hour that changes now to then;
but agency becomes, like winter skies,
obscure, and dying memory grows cold;
but bells ring on alone without surprise,
their metal tongues still strong when flesh is old;
and so the bells were each and every one
created once as slaves, but then rebelled and won.

Service Area

A Bentley sits disdainful side by side
with Hondas, Minis, even common vans,
and in each one the travelling folk who ride:
the bankers, gangsters, kids and ageing grans.
Inside the Gaming Lounge are murky booths
where errant vicars press their naughty knobs
while seated right beside addicted youths,
and in the vegan café sound the sobs
of thwarted toddlers not allowed a sweet,
but in the Gents the uncouth football fans
wee next to toffs, so brogues and trainers meet
and clarets mix with lager in the pans.
Their fellow humans always seem so strange,
in this disturbing place of ceaseless change.

Stock Exchange

Investment is a wide and stormy sea
where prices toss and bounce like drifting planks;
the managers are seamen (paid a fee)
on leaky boats with empty fuel tanks.
The storm drives shares and bonds like things possessed
while mariner investors try to snatch
their profits when they ride up on the crest:
the weaker nets come back without a catch.
The brave and sturdy steer away from rocks
through falling dollars, floating rates and scrips
across the shoals of rights and pools of stocks,
and you can cross the seas in your stout ships:
but ponder well before you scull across
that one man's profit is another's loss.

Sandwich-eaters

The shades of brokers past can be discerned
by those with patience who will search about,
yet living office-folk are not concerned
with history, but with stomachs crying out.
In London's Royal Exchange they eat their lunch
beneath imposing paintings of the great,
together on the polished seats they munch
as if collectively to ruminate:
'let us alone, time driveth onward fast'
they seem to say, and soon the clock will strike
a dreadful end, the lunch-hour will be past
again for lovers and unloved alike.
The sandwich-eaters need this tranquil place—
replete, they leave it to a silent race.

Traffic Joy

You hide inside a glass and metal cage
not strong enough to save your flimsy life,
and sometimes feel the raw red pang of rage
when drivers make lewd gestures at your wife.
They're rude extensions of their loved machines,
inhuman as a piston or a wheel.
Such folk at home may not be cruel or mean
but stuck in traffic that's the way they feel.
Once hooting starts it fast becomes a din
as drivers shut in cabins lose their calm
and try to fight a war they cannot win.
There does remain one temper-cooling balm:
since, if the traffic makes your patience wilt
you *can* enjoy being idle without guilt.

Under a Spell of Shyness

She haunts the bedroom window every day,
her alter egos lost in dustbin bags;
she's now the only actor in a play
where nothing happens, every minute drags.
She fears a footstep right outside her door
of no-one going nowhere on the stairs
for refuge on a non-existent floor
where desperate people hide away their cares.
Her neighbour waits in vain for minor treats—
an unexpected letter or the chance
to spot a passing police car in the streets;
despair is too much effort in his trance.
Although divided only by a wall
a spell of shyness holds them in its thrall.

Urban Cyclist

His gritted teeth and dark fixated glare
intimidate all rivals on the street.
He doesn't even have the time to stare
at kids he nearly knocks right off their feet.
He steams along in gleaming Lycra shorts,
his helmet like a high speed crested newt;
on hills he pedals fast with grunts and snorts,
his fierce demeanour anything but cute.
A rusty Raleigh leaves him quite non-plussed—
he hates the wobbly, slow and old, and views
electric bikes with pity and disgust:
if blocked on cycle paths he blows a fuse.
He greets all cars and walkers with dismay
but specially other cyclists in the way.

Vegan Restaurant

The pomegranate soup is very fine,
to follow, sautéed hawthorn leaves with spice
accompanied by home-made beetroot wine,
and, for dessert, a rose and tulip ice.
The whole woke menu fashioned just to please
a hirsute hipster, specially as all cooked
by gender-neutral folk in dungarees,
so popular they're always fully booked.
Is there a philosophical mistake?
When filled with tender pity they contrive
to think it wrong to eat a chop or steak—
are not the plants also as much alive?
The virtuous vegans won't touch meat or cheese,
but still eat once-live beans and peas.

Acknowledgements

Under a Spell of Shyness was first published in The Alchemy Spoon, Issue 3: *Spell*, April 2021, and *Traffic Joy* and *Delivery Driver* were first published in Sibling Poets, in 2021.

I should like to thank my wife, Harriet, for her support and benign tolerance of my writing activities. Mick Escott has encouraged me with his friendly and helpful criticism, as have many other friends too numerous to mention.

All images in this book are published free of copyright restriction under the Creative Commons CC0 1.0 Universal Public Domain Dedication, except for the image of the beggar, where the author is Shando and the file is licensed under the Creative Commons Attribution-Share Alike 2.0 Generic license.